WORLD ISSUES

ENERGY CRISIS

A look at the way the world is today

Ewan McLeish

Franklin Watts
London • Sydney

ABOUT THIS BOOK

ENERGY CRISIS? Are we facing one and what exactly does it mean? Are we going to run out of energy supplies in the next few decades, or will there be new sources of energy? If we keep on using fossil fuels at the present rate, will we soon be facing a future in which rising sea levels and freak weather dominate our lives? These are some of the issues you can read about in this book. You will also find out about what the world is doing to prevent an energy crisis and, just as importantly, how you can be involved.

© Aladdin Books Ltd 2005
Produced by
Aladdin Books Ltd
2/3 Fitzroy Mews
London W1T 6DF

ISBN 0–7496–6265–4
First published in Great Britain in 2005 by
Franklin Watts
96 Leonard Street
London EC2A 4XD

Designers: Pete Bennett – PBD
Flick, Book Design and Graphics
Editor: Harriet Brown
Picture Researcher: Alexa Brown
The author, Dr Ewan McLeish, is a writer and lecturer in education. He has written over 20 books on science and the environment. He was formerly Director of the Council for Environmental Education.
The consultant, Rob Bowden, is an education consultant, author and photographer specialising in social and environmental issues.

Printed in Malaysia

2

CONTENTS

INTRODUCTION

In August 2003, the worst power failure the world had ever seen struck the eastern part of North America. The failure hit suddenly at around 4 o'clock in the afternoon. About 50 million people in cities from New York in the United States to Toronto in Canada were affected. People were trapped in elevators and in subway (underground) trains. Computer networks shut down. As nightfall approached, New York police were put on alert to prevent looting. What had gone wrong?

A COMPLICATED ANSWER

It was a combination of events that did the damage. It was a hot day, air conditioning systems were switched on everywhere and the demand for electricity rose. This in itself should not have been a problem. But then engineers made mistakes in using the computer software that controlled the energy supply. Power lines began to shut down, voltages began to swing wildly and more lines closed. Soon the system was out of control. Ontario, in Canada, New York, and six other US states were powerless.

Energy breakdown?

This was not the only time something like this had happened. In the same year, countries in Europe including Sweden, Denmark, Italy and England all suffered major power failures.
In China, 23 of its 31 provinces (regions) had to ration power, and factories changed their production to night-time and weekends to avoid using electricity at peak times.
Something appeared to be happening to power supplies around the world.

In just three minutes, 21 power plants shut down leaving 50 million people without power.

Four devastating hurricanes hit Florida in the summer of 2004. This was the costliest hurricane season in Florida's history.

STORM WARNING

In September 2004, Hurricane Jeanne hit the coast of Florida. Hurricanes in this part of the world are common, but this was the first time four hurricanes had hit the state in a single year. Jeanne was the fourth and was stronger than the previous hurricane that had crossed the state only 20 days earlier. Jeanne blew away tarpaulins stretched across the already-damaged roofs, and ripped away any remaining roofs. Before settling on Florida, Jeanne had killed over 1,000 people as it brought torrential rains and floods to the poverty-stricken island of Haiti. Something strange seemed to be happening to the weather.

ARE THESE TWO EVENTS CONNECTED?

We know we are using energy, particularly fossil fuels, at a rapid rate. Soon there may not be enough energy available in the world to supply our needs. We are approaching an energy supply crisis.

We also know there is a connection between our use of energy and the state of the environment. We know that burning fossil fuels produces damaging waste products. We have become familiar with terms like global warming and climate change. Many believe we are at the start of a period of dramatic change in global weather – an environmental energy crisis.

CRISIS – WHAT CRISIS?

What we don't know is exactly how much of our fossil fuel supplies are left. We don't know how difficult it will be to obtain them, or how we will replace them when they run out. We also don't know how damaging our continued use of fossil fuels will be.

But we do know that solving one of these crises could also be the key to answering the other. Like so many things in this world, problems – and their solutions – are often interconnected.

This book explores the two faces of the energy crisis; how we will obtain our energy supplies in the future, and how we might do this without plunging our world into an environmental nightmare.

5

SOME FOR US – NONE FOR YOU

In 2004, a television programme about a fictional UK energy crisis was broadcast in the UK. In the programme, a combination of events created massive power cuts across the country. Transport ground to a halt, industry was crippled, the government teetered on the brink of collapse. Was the programme realistic or was it just good TV? The experts could not agree! Most of us are not experts – but we all use energy; we are all involved.

In developed countries, an incredible amount of energy is used to heat and light homes, run vehicles and keep industry functioning.

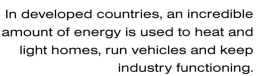

A tale of two cities

Jan, Norway – Jan lives in a big stone and wood house in Oslo, Norway. The 14-year-old is woken at 7.00 am by his radio-alarm. He gets out of bed into the thermostatically-controlled warmth of his bedroom. He looks out of the window. It is still quite dark but he can make out the white blanket of snow that has fallen overnight. No chance of missing school, though; the snowploughs will have been out long before dawn clearing the roads. And anyway, his parents' powerful, four-wheeled-drive car will make easy work of the snow. He hits the light switch, showers and dresses quickly before going downstairs to eat some cereal and hot toast. He half-hears something on the television in the next room. Something about a girl called Mala...

Mala, Somalia – Mala lives in a corrugated iron shack in Mogadishu, Somalia. The 13-year-old is woken by the light creeping between the metal sheets – that, and hunger. There isn't much to eat – some rice saved from the previous day. Mala is the eldest child, so she will have to cook it. Her mother is ill and her father away looking for work. She needs wood for the small, smoky stove in the middle of the floor. Wood is hard to come by in these parts. Battered lorries, loaded with illegal timber, sometimes roll into the city from the retreating forests, but the price is high – very high. Perhaps one of the drivers will feel sorry for her, or she might be able to pick up some fallen sticks as the lorries bump over the rutted tracks. She dreams of the day she might leave this place, maybe even own her own TV...

SPOT THE DIFFERENCE

Two very different stories about young people. Look at Jan's story again. How many times is energy involved? Six times? Seven? Eight? Actually it's more than that when you think about all the ways energy is required to make or supply the things that Jan needs or uses.

Now compare this with Mala's story. Energy is no less an important part of her life. In many ways it dominates every part of it. But the amount and type of energy used by these two young people is so different it's as though they lived on different planets, which, in many ways, they do.

Electricity consumption – country per person
(selected countries; kWh = kilowatt hours)

Country	kWh
Iceland	26,143
Norway	25,362
Canada	15,661
Sweden	15,194
Finland	14,676
United Arab Emirates	14,126
Kuwait	13,416
Luxembourg	13,365
United States	12,406
New Zealand	8,827
Belgium	7,598
Japan	7,579
Switzerland	7,301
France	6,901

In developing countries of the world energy is no less important than in developed countries. However, the amounts of energy used are tiny in comparison.

POWER TO THE PEOPLE?

Look at the table of annual electricity consumption (above). You may be surprised who comes first and second in the list – Iceland and Norway. Both are cold countries, with long, dark nights for long periods of the year. Both can produce electricity fairly cheaply because they are able to tap into large quantities of hydroelectric power from their many rivers and lakes.

Perhaps also surprisingly, the United States only comes ninth in the list of electricity guzzlers. The average American only uses about half the electricity of the average Norwegian, but this is still over twice as much as the average Briton or German.

At the other end of the scale, the average person in Afghanistan uses only 18 kWh. In Somalia, Mala only uses about one four-hundredth of the electricity used by the average American. That's about enough to run a single light bulb for one hour a day – if she had one.

7

THE HAVES AND THE HAVE NOTS

Energy comes in many forms and electricity is only one of them. Poor countries often cannot afford to build or run power stations or transport the electricity over great distances along power lines. This is especially true in rural areas. They often rely on forms of energy such as wood, kerosene or animal dung.

Look at the chart below – the OECD (Organisation for Economic Co-operation and Development) countries – rich regions like North America, Western Europe and Japan – dominate the picture, with Eastern Europe and the former Soviet Union coming way behind. Now look at Africa's line. It is easy to see who are the energy haves and have nots.

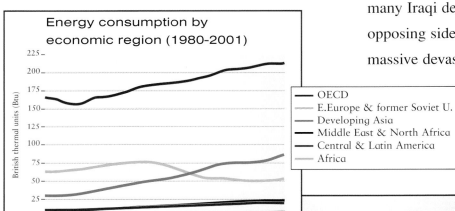

Energy consumption by economic region (1980-2001)

British thermal units (Btu)

OECD
E.Europe & former Soviet U.
Developing Asia
Middle East & North Africa
Central & Latin America
Africa

WEAPON OF MASS DEVASTATION?

In 1990, Iraq invaded its tiny southern neighbour Kuwait. Whatever excuses were made for the attack, there was only one real reason – oil. Iraq was already a big producer of oil, but its leader, Saddam Hussein, wanted more. Kuwait has huge oil reserves. Controlling Kuwait's oil, as well as his own, would give Saddam enormous power in the region, perhaps in the world. And power was what he craved.

A coalition of countries, including the US and Britain, decided that Saddam had to be stopped. They went to war to drive his troops out of Kuwait.

It was a short, but bitter and bloody war, with many Iraqi deaths, as well as casualties on the opposing side. Kuwait was liberated but there was massive devastation of its oil wells and installations, as the Iraqi army retreated. Oil fires burned for months, sending plumes of

As a result of the Gulf War, over 700 oil wells were damaged. Of these, more than 600 were set on fire. Over 1,200 km of coastline were covered with oil.

black, poisonous smoke into the upper atmosphere. Much of the Persian Gulf was polluted, as oil from broken pipelines seeped into its clear blue waters.

Perhaps for the first time, and certainly not the last, the world's most important source of energy – oil – had become something to fight a war over.

Driven by energy

Now Saddam's reign in Iraq is over. But the conflicts still go on. Oil prices are rising as many of the world's oil producers face internal and external threats. Terrorism and the possibility of sabotage of pipelines and oil installations, haunt world governments.

It's an oil thing

We have seen that there are huge differences in the amount of energy used by different parts of the world. We have also seen that energy resources, particularly oil, have become so important that countries are prepared to go to war over them. In a sense, oil has become a weapon used by different countries or groups to exert control over others.

At the same time, countries are desperate to safeguard their own energy supplies. Many nations cannot meet their own energy needs and have to buy it from other countries. They have to remain friendly with those countries. 'Security of supply' has become one of the most important issues to emerge at the beginning of the 21st century. Some people think the main reason America and its allies removed Saddam from power in 2003 was to protect their own oil interests. Others disagree.

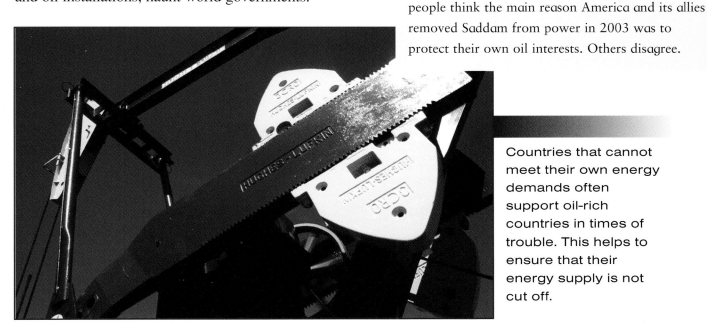

Countries that cannot meet their own energy demands often support oil-rich countries in times of trouble. This helps to ensure that their energy supply is not cut off.

Taking it for granted?

Finally, we need to remind ourselves that not everyone in the richer countries has unlimited energy at the touch of a button. Even in rich societies there are groups – the unemployed or the elderly, for example – who often find it hard to meet their winter heating bills.

But we also need to understand that being able to use large amounts of energy is not always the same as having a good 'quality of life'. Many people lead rich lives on much less energy than most of us reading this book.

Whatever we think, we may all have to get used to the idea that energy is no longer something we can take for granted.

GOOD FUELS OR BAD NEIGHBOURS

In April 1986, a safety test at a nuclear reactor in Chernobyl, Ukraine, went disastrously wrong. One of the reactors overheated, causing a massive explosion that blew radioactive material high into the atmosphere. Much of eastern and northern Europe was contaminated. We do not know how many people will eventually die of thyroid and other cancers as a result. Areas close to the reactor are still too radioactive for people to return.

The force of the explosion at Chernobyl spread contamination over large parts of the former Soviet Union and Europe.

Solar power is one of the more well-known sources of renewable energy.

You will probably be familiar with the terms, 'renewable' and 'non-renewable' energy. Renewable energy is energy we can use without depleting (exhausting) the original resource. Wind, wave, solar and some types of hydroelectric power and biofuels (wood, charcoal and crop residues) are renewable sources of energy. Fossil fuels, on the other hand, are non-renewable and we're using them up rapidly. They also tend to be more polluting. Nuclear power is non-renewable, although it will take a long time to use up all the uranium fuel available.

This chapter looks at these non-renewable resources. It includes large-scale hydroelectric schemes since, like fossil fuels and nuclear power, they can be good sources of energy – but bad neighbours!

FOSSIL RECORD

We have relied on fossil fuels for thousands of years. Fossil fuels are a dependable and 'concentrated' source of energy. This means we can get large quantities of useful energy from them. Fossil fuels are easy to store and transport. Compared to other forms of energy, they are also fairly cheap, although that is likely to change as they become less plentiful.

When fossil fuels are burned, they release harmful chemicals into the atmosphere.

THE GLOBAL PICTURE

We still get most of our energy from fossil fuels, either using them directly (such as petrol or diesel in cars) or by producing electricity in power stations. Look at the chart on the right. You will see that, in the rich regions of the world, oil alone provides nearly 50% of total energy use. Coal and gas come in joint second at around 20% each. That's nearly 90% of energy use accounted for by fossil fuels.

In poorer countries, the 'mix' appears to be similar (although the rich countries use six times more fossil fuel overall). Oil is still first, but coal comes a close second. The chart only shows commercial energy, though – energy that is bought and sold. Millions of people in poorer countries depend on wood for fuel; energy that does not appear on most balance sheets.

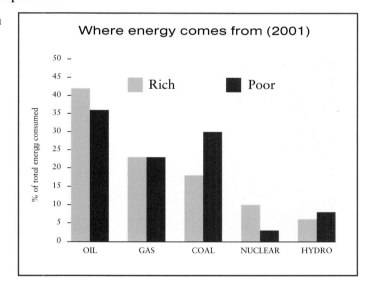

Where energy comes from (2001)

11

The problem with fossils

The problem with fossil fuels is that burning them releases a combination of harmful or dangerous gases into the atmosphere. We think one of these – carbon dioxide – is causing the temperature of the Earth's atmosphere to increase. We also think this may be causing the Earth's climate to change and sea levels to rise.

There are other problems attached to our use of fossil fuels. Extracting them from the ground or under the seabed can also be damaging and dangerous. In 2004 alone, 1,000 Chinese miners died in mining accidents. Oil spills at sea can kill marine life and devastate coastlines for decades. Oil pipelines can disrupt the migration routes of animals such as caribou. As supplies of fossil fuels dwindle (pages 18-23), the pressure to drill for oil in fragile ecosystems such as Alaska may become irresistible. And as we have already seen, many of the countries rich in fossil fuels, such as Iraq and Saudi Arabia, are politically unstable. Recently, oil pipelines have been attacked by groups who want to destabilise (unsettle) these countries further.

GOING NUCLEAR

When atoms of uranium or other radioactive isotopes are split, the tiny amount of energy holding each atom together is released as heat. Splitting atoms creates a chain reaction involving more and more atoms. Eventually, vast amounts of heat energy are released. This turns water into steam, which drives turbines attached to generators, producing electricity.

Nuclear power stations provide an important portion of the world's energy. However, nuclear power is expensive and can be dangerous.

12

Too good to be true?

When nuclear power first became available in the 1950s, most people thought electricity would be 'too cheap to meter'. Uranium was not in short supply and some of the used uranium could be recycled as plutonium and used in different ('fast breeder') reactors. What is more, nuclear power produces very little in the way of greenhouse gases, such as carbon dioxide.

Instead of being cheap, nuclear power turned out to be far more expensive than predicted; far more than coal or oil. Then there were concerns about safety. What would happen if there were an accident and radioactive material escaped? What if nuclear materials were stolen by a terrorist group and made into nuclear weapons?

A problem waiting to happen

There are over 443 nuclear power stations world-wide, in over 30 different countries. The United States has 104, Armenia has one. The country most dependent on nuclear power is Lithuania. By 2012, over 200 nuclear installations will need to be decommissioned (see below). A safe way of doing this has yet to be agreed.

Going, going but not gone

Fortunately, accidents, like the one at Chernobyl, are rare. But the problem of disposing of large amounts of radioactive waste remains. Some will be dangerous for thousands, even millions of years and even if this problem is solved, many nuclear power stations will soon become too old to operate safely. 'Decommissioning' (making them safe) will be both costly and dangerous.

In the richer countries, about 10% of total energy (and about 17% of electricity) is supplied by nuclear power. In the rest of the world, nuclear power makes a smaller (but important) contribution. Because of the cost and possible dangers, many countries are planning to close down their nuclear programmes.

However, 27 nuclear reactors are being built, including eight in India, four in the Ukraine, three in Russia, two in Iran and two in North Korea. Some of these are not the most politically stable areas in the world!

Meanwhile, as the energy crisis bites more deeply, some of the countries about to abandon their nuclear power programmes, such as the UK, are having second thoughts.

RIVER BUSTERS

On the 3rd November 2002, the natural flow of China's Yangtze River stopped forever. The river began flowing out of 22 concrete holes towards the enormous dam that would one-day supply 10% of China's power and control the annual floods that had killed millions of people.

Hydroelectric power uses the energy contained in the water cycle. This often involves the construction of huge dams, creating giant lakes that supply the pressure required to turn the massive turbine blades.

Big or what!

The Three Gorges Dam, being built on China's giant Yangtze River, is nearly 2.5 km long and 200 m high. It will create a lake 640 km in length and cause over a million people to be resettled. The dam will use 26.4 million cubic metres of concrete – enough to cover a football pitch to a height of 5 km! It should produce the same amount of electricity as 18 nuclear power stations. The project is due for completion in 2009.

Dams deliver?

Hydroelectricity can provide large quantities of energy in a useful form. It is important to both rich and poor countries, supplying a sixth of the world's electricity. In countries like Egypt, it has brought the benefits of electricity to thousands of isolated villages and communities. Hydroelectric power stations have low running costs and produce few greenhouse or other gases. In theory, at least, they have a longer life than fossil fuel or nuclear power stations. They can also help control flooding and discourage people from cutting down trees for fuel.

Renewable or not renewable

Constructing giant dams, however, is a hugely expensive business, using up vast amounts of building material, as well as energy itself! Often the electricity they produce goes to big cities, rather than benefiting local communities.

Dams flood hundreds of square kilometres of land. Often this is farmland or unspoiled forest inhabited by rare or important species. At the same time, farmland downstream of the dam is deprived of nutrients brought by seasonal floods. In many cases, hundreds or thousands of local communities have to be moved. Dams have a limited useful life. The lakes start to fill up with silt and the dams become less efficient. The flooded forests decompose, producing greenhouse gases such as methane and carbon dioxide.

Local people are often priced out of the newly available energy produced by hydroelectric dams. They are forced to continue to deplete local forests to meet their energy requirements.

13

ENERGY WITHOUT END

In the hills above San Francisco is a race of giants. Over 100 m tall, their great blade-like arms move slowly in the steady breeze. As you move closer, you can hear them murmur and hum. Once their ancestors ground corn; now the great blades produce a different commodity – electricity.

At Altamont Pass, near San Francisco, USA, 6,000 wind turbines generate electricity. However, the wind farm is not popular with many people as it is thought to harm birds, in particular the golden eagle.

EFFICIENT AND CHEAP?

Wind power is one of the fastest-growing renewable energy technologies in the world. By 2003, a total of 31,000 megawatts had been installed world-wide; that's about the same as 30 nuclear power stations. Modern wind turbines are efficient, cheap to run and easy to maintain.

14

Global wind capacity at the end of 2002

Region	Capacity (megawatts)
Europe	23,291
North America	4,923
Asia, Pacific, South America	2,914
GLOBAL TOTAL	31,128

Europe dominates the global wind power capacity league, producing nearly three-quarters of the world total. The global total is over 31 gigawatts.

Two large turbines installed at Swaffham, UK, provide about 70% of the town's electricity needs – that's enough for nearly 2,000 homes.

Many people still object to wind turbines because of their appearance and noise. Better designs mean that noise levels are now lower. Even so, growing opposition means that offshore sites, where winds are higher and more reliable, may be more suitable. Here, however, there is concern about the impact on navigation and marine life, especially migrating sea birds. It is still too early to say how serious this problem will be.

SOLAR CELLS

We can use the Sun as an energy source by gathering its heat energy directly (solar heating) or by converting its radiation into electricity, using solar or photovoltaic (PV) cells.

A single photovoltaic cell produces about 1.5 watts of electricity (a light bulb is about 60 watts). To obtain more power, groups of cells are connected together to form arrays. A growing number of buildings now have PV arrays providing significant

amounts of electrical energy. More recently, a number of large, megawatt-sized (million watt) PV power stations, connected to electricity grids, have been operating in the USA and Europe.

PV cells are expensive to produce and work best in direct sunlight. They have no moving parts, however, so maintenance is low. PV cells have been described as 'the ideal energy conversion system' (pages 30-33).

HARNESSING THE SEA

Wave power is almost unlimited. There are many different designs of generator, some fixed to the shore, others floating. Most work by compressing air, water or other liquid, which operates a turbine. In the now famous 'duck' design, the movement of the waves rocks large floating, jointed drums which drive the turbine. Prototype wave energy extractors have been built near or on coastlines in many parts of the world.

Capturing the energy of the tides goes back to the Middle Ages. More recently, tidal energy has been used to generate electricity, with turbines mounted on large 'barrages' built across estuaries.

There have been proposals for truly massive barrages with several gigawatts (billion watts) of capacity. One would cross the Severn Estuary in the UK. If built, it would be 16 km across and could supply 5% of the UK's electricity!

Large barrages, however, do have drawbacks. They have a big impact on the estuaries on which they are built. Estuaries usually have large mud flats exposed at low tide, which are important feeding sites for wildfowl. By trapping the tide, the mud flats are altered and the birds' feeding patterns disturbed.

15

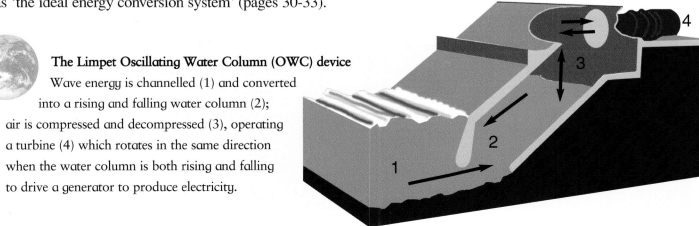

The Limpet Oscillating Water Column (OWC) device
Wave energy is channelled (1) and converted into a rising and falling water column (2); air is compressed and decompressed (3), operating a turbine (4) which rotates in the same direction when the water column is both rising and falling to drive a generator to produce electricity.

SMALL DAMS BEAT THEIR BIG COUSINS?

Not all hydroelectric schemes are on such a
massive scale as the Three Gorges Dam, described
on page 13. Small dams already produce up to a
third of China's electricity. They do less damage
and the electricity they produce does not have to
be carried vast distances along power
lines. Norway's mountainous landscape
and many rivers enable it to produce
95% of its electricity without the need
to build large dams. Other countries
with mountainous terrain and poor
electricity supplies, such as Nepal,
could also benefit from the construction
of small-scale schemes.

MINING HEAT FROM THE GROUND

In some parts of the world, the Earth's
heat is concentrated enough to produce hot water and
steam at temperatures between 180 and 250°C. This
geothermal energy can be harnessed to drive turbines
or supply heating systems. Perhaps surprisingly, the
country with the most geothermal power generation

High temperature geothermal
reservoirs are the ones suitable for
commercial production of electricity at
geothermal power plants.

is the US, followed closely by the Philippines
and then Mexico (see the table, below left).

New technology is now becoming available
(known as 'Hot Dry Rock') which does not
require natural water to be present. Cold water
is pumped into the hot rock and then returned,
heated. The technology is complicated,
however, and still mostly at the research stage.

At the other end of the scale, ground source
heat pumps (GSHPs) extract heat at only 12-
15°C from depths of 100-150 m. Although
they only deliver a few kilowatts, there are
now thousands of individual units
providing energy to homes in Europe, and
over 400,000 in the US.

Geothermal power generation – top 5 countries

Country	Output (2000)	Output (2005) est.
USA	2,228 mW	2,376 mW
Philippines	1,909 mW	2,673 mW
Mexico	855 mW	1,080 mW
Italy	785 mW	946 mW
Indonesia	590 mW	1,987 mW

mW = Megawatts
1,000 Megawatts = 1 large coal or
nuclear power station

16

In Brazil, it is estimated that the production of ethanol from sugar cane has saved fossil fuel imports of US $40 billion, and 13 million tonnes of carbon emissions a year. In recent years, increased oil production and poor harvests have threatened the industry.

BIOENERGY – THE ENERGY OF LIFE

Bioenergy is energy obtained from materials, such as wood, straw or animal wastes, that were recently living matter (biomass). This material can be burned directly or converted into biofuels, such as biodiesel or ethanol (alcohol). In many poorer countries, wood still accounts for up to a third of energy consumption. Collecting it can contribute to the destruction of forests and desertification of land. Burning wastes such as animal dung deprives small farmers of natural fertilisers.

The term 'new biomass' has come into use and describes materials that are processed on a large, commercial scale. These may come from crops grown for the purpose or from waste material such as straw or 'municipal waste'. They may produce useful heat or solid, liquid or gas fuels.

In theory, biofuels are 'carbon neutral'. So, as long as they are replaced, the carbon they release during combustion is equal to the carbon they previously absorbed from the atmosphere while growing. However, this replacement does not always happen!

A QUESTION OF CONTROL

Renewable energy technologies can be built to supply local communities. They do not need large, centralised generating stations or distribution systems. Once built, the source of energy is free. The consumers are no longer dependent on outside sources of energy, such as oil. They are in control of their own energy supplies.

Finally, it is easy to fall into the trap of thinking of non-renewable fuels as 'bad' and renewables as 'good'. This would be a dangerous oversimplification. All energy comes at a cost and we have to learn how to weigh these costs against the benefits they bring.

17

Wood is used as a source of bioenergy. However, this is often not a 'carbon neutral' energy source.

AN ENERGY BLACK HOLE?

In June 2004, China released figures showing its crude oil imports had soared by nearly 40% in the first half of the year. Meanwhile, China's stockpile of coal plunged to its lowest level in 20 years. Its electricity system was also under strain, with demand up by 15% from the previous year. Power cuts sent waves of darkness across the giant country. So, is China, and the rest of the world, about to run out of fuel?

WHERE DOES IT COME FROM?

In the first chapter, we looked at the consumers of energy – the energy guzzlers and the energy have nots. Now we need to look at the producers, the countries and regions who supply and, importantly, control the flow of energy around the world.

Look at the chart (left), which shows production by source of energy. It is rather similar to the consumption chart on page 11. Not surprisingly, it is dominated by oil and other fossil fuels. Nuclear and hydroelectric power come equal fourth, with various types of renewable energy last. Renewables account for only about 1.5% of total production.

World energy production by source (2002)

Y-axis: Quadrillion (10⁹) Btu

Values (approximate): Crude oil 150, Coal 100, Natural gas 95, Nuclear electric power 27, Hydro-electric power 28, Geothermal and other renewable sources 7

Coal is the second most widely used source of energy. It is a fossil fuel and its burning releases carbon dioxide into the atmosphere.

Now look at energy production by region (below). As we might predict, the Americas are well in the lead, followed by Asia and Oceania, and then Eastern Europe and the former Soviet Union. It is interesting to look at Western Europe as, although a big consumer, it is a relatively low producer. This means it is very dependent on other regions to meet its energy needs. Once again, Africa is not a large energy producer, at least for its size.

The USA is the leading energy producer in the world, followed by Russia and China. As we shall see, both have enormous deposits of coal; Russia is also rich in natural gas. Fourth in the league comes the oil-rich state of Saudi Arabia. Perhaps surprisingly, the UK comes high up the league in sixth place. This is likely to change as its offshore oil and gas deposits run down.

Saudi Arabia is the number one producer of oil. Other Middle Eastern states, such as Iran, the UAE and Kuwait, also figure strongly.

Middle Eastern states produce more oil than any other region of the world.

ENERGY = CONTROL = POWER?

Many of the world's leading oil nations belong to a powerful group called the Oil and Petroleum Exporting Countries (OPEC). They control the supply of about half the world's oil.

Look at the price of oil between 1970 and 2004 (see page 20). Until the early '70s oil was cheap but in 1973, the price rose dramatically.

Why this price rise? Fears that oil might be running out suddenly gripped the world. The oil producers realised they were literally sitting on a product with which they could rule the world. From now on they would control the rate of production, and with that, they would control the price. Since that time, price has varied widely and at the time of writing this book, the price of oil is higher than ever.

Production has also increased so that, on a world basis, it is higher than ever before. But fears about security of supply and instability in many oil-producing countries, still keep production in check and prices high.

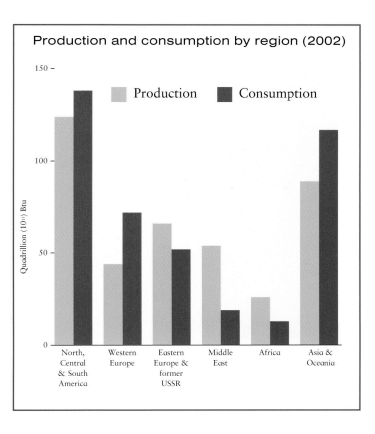

Production and consumption by region (2002)

Quadrillion (10^{15}) Btu

Production | Consumption

North, Central & South America | Western Europe | Eastern Europe & former USSR | Middle East | Africa | Asia & Oceania

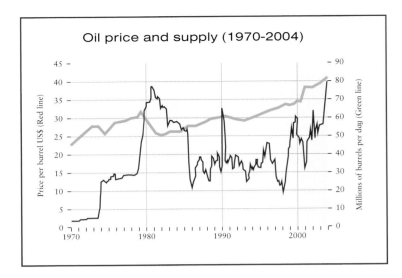

Oil price and supply (1970-2004)

WHERE DOES IT GO?

We have looked at how much energy is consumed by different countries and regions. Now we need to think about the different uses that energy is put to.

If we look at the US, we find that the greatest user of energy is industry (38%). Almost equal in importance, however, is residential and commercial use (35%). This means energy used for homes and offices. The final big energy user is transport. Over a quarter (27%) of energy consumed in the US goes on moving people and goods around.

GETTING AROUND

In Denmark, as in most of Europe, by far the greatest user of energy is road transport – cars and lorries. Rail and sea use far smaller amounts of energy. Perhaps the most surprising is air transport, which comes second only to road transport in terms of energy use. Between 1970 and 2000, the energy consumed by road users increased by 50% in Denmark.

If you were to look at Western Europe as a whole, you would discover that 85% of the energy used in moving people around goes into cars. Only 2.5% and 3.5% of transport energy goes into buses and railways. When you look at the number of journeys,

Industry is a massive consumer of energy, particularly in developed nations.

however, you will see that nearly 7% are made by bus and nearly 30% are made by train! You can see that buses and trains are a far more energy-efficient way of getting around than cars.

The same is true for moving goods or freight. In Europe, 98% of all building materials and manufactured products, 97% of foods, 95% of agricultural products and 75% of oil products go by road, rather than rail. In purely energy terms, however, transporting goods by rail is nearly five times more efficient.

20

DRIVING INDUSTRY

About 70% of energy used in European industry goes into manufacturing. The next biggest industrial energy consumers are agriculture (farming) and the construction (building) industry. As we have seen, even obtaining energy itself requires that large amounts of energy are used.

The picture is very different world-wide. Agriculture dominates the economies of many poorer countries. This is often dependent on animal or people power, rather than machinery. As we have seen, many of the poorer regions are now moving into the industrial age and becoming the new manufacturing nations of the world. And that means their energy needs are soaring.

ENERGY AT HOME

Look back at Jan's story on page 6. He uses many forms of energy in a day. A typical European home uses about 60 kilowatt hours of energy a day. That's like boiling an electric kettle 24 hours a day! Most of this is used in heating (below, left). About 40% of the energy comes from gas, 33% from electricity and the rest from kerosene and other sources. Much of the electricity comes from power stations fuelled either by oil, gas or coal.

Now think back to the story about Mala. Her energy use is a fraction of that of Jan's. Most is supplied by wood or kerosene and is burned inefficiently, wasting energy and releasing harmful chemicals.

Space heating
58%

Cooking 5%

Lights and appliances
13%

Water heating
24%

Here we can see where the energy is used in a typical home in a European country.

AN ENERGY BLACK HOLE?

So are we running out of energy? Will we use up our supplies of fossil fuels before we can find sufficient alternatives?

To answer these questions, we first need to look at our energy reserves; how much we think we still have left. Look at the chart on the next page for oil and natural gas reserves. By far the most crude oil remains in the Middle East. The Americas have some oil reserves but far less than the Middle East. Not that much remains elsewhere. For natural gas, the picture is rather different. The Middle East comes out on top, but there are still large reserves in the former Soviet Union and Eastern Europe. Western Europe has little of either left.

Coal reserves are distributed between North America, the former Soviet Union/Eastern Europe, and the Middle East and Asia. Western Europe also has a good supply. The top five countries are the US, followed by Russia, China, India and Australia.

21

Most of the energy used for your home and school appliances comes in the form of electricity generated by power stations using oil, gas or coal.

HOW LONG WILL IT LAST?

If you add up the total figures for oil reserves, you will find they come to about 1,147 billion barrels. This is pretty hard to imagine, but it sounds a lot! The consumption rate for oil is about 75 million barrels a day or 27,375 million barrels a year! That's around 27 billion. So now all you need to do is divide 1,147 by 27 and you have the number of years of oil we have left – if we go on using it at the present rate. As you will see, it's not that long.

We can carry out similar calculations for coal and gas. In fact, most estimates now suggest that oil will last for about another 40 years, natural gas for 70 years and coal for 190 years.

Of course, estimating amounts of fuel in the ground is not easy. We normally talk about 'known' reserves. There may be others we don't know about. As fossil fuels become scarcer (and therefore more valuable) it may become economically viable to extract sources that were previously not considered worthwhile. Exploration and extraction methods are

If we go on using oil at today's rate, it is likely to run out in your lifetime.

22

also getting better all the time. And as we just saw, these estimates are also based on the present rate of consumption. If we use less, they will last longer!

On the other hand, the estimates assume we can go on getting our reserves out of the ground at the same rate as now. As they become scarcer, supply is likely to slow down. It looks as though peak production of oil will occur in the next 10 years, and gas in the next 30 years. After that time, they will be harder to obtain.

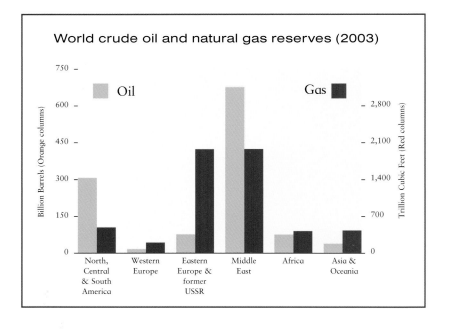

Telling the future

All the evidence suggests that the two most important fossil fuels – oil and gas – will run out or become scarce in 50 years or so, maybe less. Since most of the known oil reserves are in the Middle East, the rest of the world will become more and more dependent on this region to meet its energy needs. This will make an already unstable part of the world still more explosive as countries try to secure their oil supplies.

This could be prevented if we use oil and gas more efficiently, and if we move away from an 'oil-based' economy to one in which other energy sources play a much larger role.

If we are to make the world a more politically stable place to live in, it is important that we move away from a fossil-fuel based economy.

This means only using fossil fuels where absolutely necessary.

So what about all that coal that still sits, in vast deposits, in many parts of the world? It is true that coal will go on being an important fuel for some time to come, especially in the rapidly developing parts of the world, such as Asia.

Coal is a 'dirty' fuel and produces more carbon dioxide than other fossil fuels. Coal could – and will – meet some of our future energy needs. But, as we shall see in the next chapter, relying on it could plunge the world not into an energy black hole, but a climatic one.

23

Even with new technologies able to get rid of some of the nastier waste products, coal still produces more carbon dioxide than gas or oil.

THE REAL ENERGY CRISIS?

On the 13th of August 2002, the hanging Kolka Glacier in southern Russia collapsed. Just over a month later, the collapse of another glacier nearby triggered an avalanche that thundered down the slopes of Mount Dzhimarai-Khokh. Ice and debris slid over 24 km, burying small villages in its path and killing dozens of people.

Although scientists had predicted the possibility of large-scale glacial collapses as the climate warmed, no one had foreseen this particular tragedy. But cameras, high above the Earth in the International Space Station, captured its path as the avalanche carved its way down the mountainside and smashed into the valleys below.

Here you can see Mount Dzhimarai-Khokh both before (left) and after (right) the collapse of the Kolka Glacier. Dozens of people were killed. These images were captured by astronauts in the International Space Station.

THE HUMAN FACTOR

Most estimates agree that global temperatures have risen by over half a degree (0.6) centigrade in the last 150 years. Many now believe the effect on world climate could be dramatic – even catastrophic. There is now evidence to suggest the increase itself is speeding up.

What people cannot agree on is the exact cause of the increase – or its likely impact. The climate is constantly changing over different periods of time. But over the past century, the rate of warming cannot easily be explained by natural variations. In 1996, a group of experts issued the following statement: "The balance of evidence suggests a discernible human influence on global climate through emissions of carbon dioxide and other greenhouse gases."

GLOBAL SHIELD

So how does global warming work? The energy (radiation) that reaches the Earth from the Sun is at short wavelengths. About 24% of this passes through the atmosphere and clouds and reaches the Earth itself. Here it heats the Earth's surface which then throws heat energy back into the atmosphere. But now it is different. This cooler (infrared) radiation has a longer wavelength. The so-called greenhouse gases, such as carbon dioxide and methane, are good at absorbing this particular wavelength. They work like a massive shield, absorbing then re-transmitting this heat energy back to Earth. The result is a warmer planet.

Normally, this is a very good thing! Naturally occurring greenhouse gases mean that the Earth operates, on average, at a reasonably comfortable 15 °C. Without them, most of the planet would be a frozen wasteland. The problems start when the levels of greenhouse gases start to rise above normal.

But what is normal?

Look at the graphs below. They show the rise in temperature and the rise in carbon dioxide concentration over the last 100 years. The lines look spookily similar, although they are to different scales. Of course, this does not necessarily mean there is a connection – other factors could be causing both to rise together. But most scientists think the two are related.

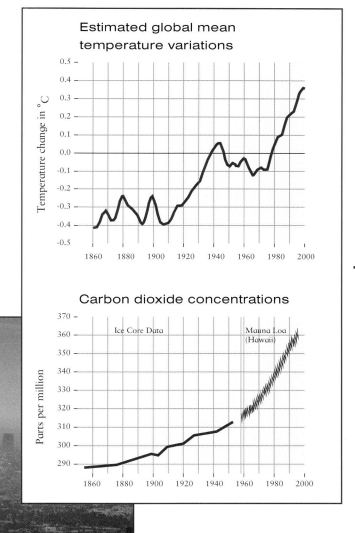

25

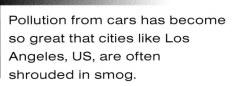

Pollution from cars has become so great that cities like Los Angeles, US, are often shrouded in smog.

Record highs

Every year we are releasing almost seven billion tonnes of carbon into the atmosphere. This is carbon that has lain buried since the days of the dinosaurs and it will now remain in the atmosphere for around a century. Before the industrial age, carbon dioxide levels were steady at around 280 parts per million (280 ppm – about 0.03%). By 1997, they had reached 368 ppm (see pages 40-43) and in 2004 they hit 379.

A 60 cm rise in sea levels would mean that cities such as Bombay, Tokyo and New York would need massive sea defences to keep back the rising water.

Runaway!

Carbon dioxide is not the only greenhouse gas – it only makes about a 50% contribution. Methane, produced by bacteria living in conditions where there is little oxygen – such as marshes and landfill sites – also has a greenhouse effect. So do gases such as nitrogen dioxide and ozone, produced by motor vehicles.

Like carbon dioxide, methane levels are also rising. It's possible that large quantities of methane, currently frozen in deep ocean beds and in Arctic tundra soils, could be released if global temperatures continue to rise. We would then get what is known as a runaway greenhouse effect.

CAUSE AND EFFECT – SEA LEVELS ON THE RISE

Sea levels have risen by about 2 cm over the last 100 years. Again, this does not sound very much, but the indications are that, even at the present rate of warming, the sea-level rise will reach 60 cm by the end of the century. Combined with more frequent storms and hurricanes, this will make many low-lying areas of the world uninhabitable.

In countries such as Bangladesh the situation is far worse. In just 50 years, a combination of sea-level rise and sinking land could mean an overall increase of 1.8 m. That would plunge 16% of the country under water. Many Pacific islands would disappear.

The main reason for the rapid increase in sea levels is the melting of ice at the two poles. A NASA satellite survey of the Arctic in 2002 showed that sea ice coverage was the lowest in 20 years of observation. Meanwhile, Antarctic glaciers are thinning at twice the rate they were in the 1990s.

The Arctic tundra contains frozen methane, which may be released if global temperatures continue to rise.

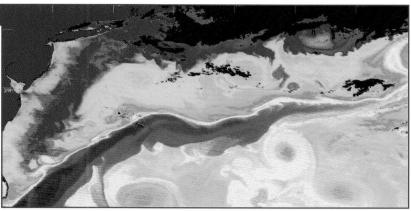

The red strip in this image indicates the Gulf Stream, a massive band of warmer water in the Atlantic Ocean.

GLOBAL FREEZING?

There is another, equally dramatic, possibility. Much of Western Europe is kept warm by the Gulf Stream, a huge ocean current that brings warm water up from the tropics. The Gulf Stream itself is kept going by a deeper current, the Conveyor, moving in the opposite direction. This current is caused by dense, saline water sinking at high northerly latitudes. As more of the icecap melts, this water will become less salty and therefore less dense. The Conveyor could slow down or stop altogether and this, in turn, will affect the Gulf Stream.

Rather than global warming, parts of the Northern Hemisphere could experience exactly the opposite effect. For example, the climate in the UK could start resembling that of Norway.

Meltdown!

In Greenland there is a high, central part of the ice sheet that never melts. The Greenland Ice Cap contains 8% of the total global ice-mass and is on average 2,135 m high. It contains around 2.5 million cubic km of ice. Over the last 30 years there has been a definite reduction in this area, particularly in the warmer south-west.

A total melting of the Greenland Ice Cap would raise sea levels a massive 7.4 m! A temperature rise of about 4°C would be enough to do this, although it would take several hundred years to occur.

WINNERS AND LOSERS?

It is likely that temperature rises will be greater at higher latitudes than nearer the equator. The paths of rain-bearing winds could change, causing a fall in crop production in large parts of the US and Europe. More northerly areas, like Canada and Scandinavia, could see agriculture expand as temperatures rise. Rates of evaporation from soils will also increase, which could mean severe water shortages in places such as China. Globally, the effects of climate change could be disastrous.

Agricultural patterns across the globe could change as a result of climate change.

Deadly chain

For centuries, the massive seabird colonies of Orkney, Fair Isle and Shetland in Northern Scotland have dominated the rocky ledges and stacks. Shetland alone has around a million seabirds. In recent years, the great colonies have begun to falter and then, in 2004, the cliffs fell eerily silent as tens of thousands of birds failed to raise any young. In 20 years the average temperature of the North Sea has risen by 2°C and as a result, cold water plankton drifted 1,000 km north. Young sandeels, which feed on the plankton, began to decline. Now the birds, which feed on the adult sandeels, have begun to decline too.

CHANGING LIVES

Habitats too will change. Insect-eating birds, like blue tits, normally produce their young to coincide with the emergence of caterpillars. Warmer springs mean the caterpillars emerge earlier – too early sometimes to be food for blue tit chicks. Natural selection may mean the birds will adapt their own breeding cycle to follow the caterpillars, but some scientists think they will not be able to change quickly enough.

On a global scale, habitats may gradually move to higher latitudes (further north and south). Some plants and animals may be able to follow these changes, but others will not.

A study by biologists in Leeds, UK, came to the conclusion that, "global warming may drive a quarter of land animals and plants to the edge of extinction by 2050". Even the 'best case scenario' predicts 9% facing extinction.

THE USUAL SUSPECTS?

So who are the main greenhouse gas producers? Take a look at carbon dioxide production by region (chart, right). Asia and Oceania are in the lead, with North America as a whole (USA, Canada and Alaska) in second place, followed by Western Europe. If you were to repeat the chart by country alone – rather than by region – you would discover that, for carbon dioxide at least, the US comes in a clear first place, followed by China and then Russia. Both China and Russia are big coal users, and coal is particularly good (or bad) at producing carbon dioxide, as well as other pollutants.

Many creatures are currently facing extinction across the globe. Global warming would serve to change their habitats and make their decline faster still. Those that can adapt will survive; those that can't will not.

Countries like China, Indonesia, Thailand and Korea are becoming big industrial players and soon they will become giants. Their energy demands are rising rapidly and most of this demand is being met by fossil fuels. Carbon dioxide production over the last 20 years by these regions of the world has increased as they too enter the industrial age.

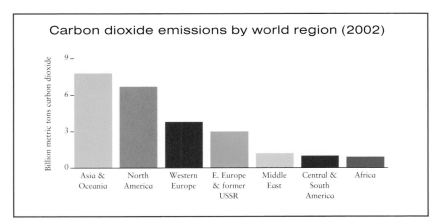

Carbon dioxide emissions by world region (2002)

We know that burning fossil fuels has other harmful effects which include the damage to forests, lakes and buildings caused by acid rain. Some progress has been made in combating acid emissions in North America and Western Europe. This involves high-temperature combustion and neutralising acid gases, such as sulphur dioxide. Switching from coal to less polluting, gas-fired power stations has also helped reduce acid levels. But as large regions of the world enter the industrial age, they will dramatically increase their use of fossil fuels. Between 1990 and 2010, sulphur dioxide emissions in Asia are set to triple.

GLOBAL WARNING?

This chapter has concentrated on the effects of global warming, caused mainly by our use of fossil fuels. Cutting down forests also has an important impact on carbon dioxide levels. As well as producing oxygen, trees store carbon dioxide, locking up large amounts of carbon for many years. Burning them releases that carbon back into the atmosphere.

THE REAL ENERGY CRISIS?

We have looked at some of the possible effects on the planet of our massive reliance on fossil fuels. There will also be a human cost – economies will suffer, global food production will be altered and societies will be disrupted. As usual, the poor of this world will be most affected since they are least able to change or control their circumstances.

So – crisis or no crisis? After all, it could all be part of the natural cycle of events, but most people are no longer willing to take that chance.

29

Acid rain damages forests and soils, fish and other living things, materials, and human health.

Doing More with Less

In most power stations, steam is used to turn a turbine, which operates a generator and produces electricity. The steam is first pressurised and then raised to around 650°C. Below 450°C the process is no longer efficient, which means that heat in waste gases below this temperature cannot be used and is lost. And this means most power stations are only about 35% efficient.

The use of heat exchangers is one way in which waste heat can be re-used. This can increase the energy efficiency of the appliance or industry.

HOW COULD WE USE THIS WASTED HEAT?

One way would be to use a liquid that vapourises (boils) at a much lower temperature than water. This would mean less energy would be required to heat the liquid and pressurise the vapour.

Surprisingly, this liquid could be a fossil fuel itself – propane. Propane has a low boiling point (around 50°C) and using propane instead of water could increase the efficiency of power stations from 35% to 60%. Waste heat would still be produced but, because of propane's low boiling point, most of this could be captured by a second turbine to produce more electricity. Gases leaving the power station could be at temperatures as low as 55°C instead of 450°C. The technology would also allow other industrial waste heat to be re-used rather than wasted.

Old ideas – new ideas?

Such technology is still experimental, but unless we develop much more efficient ways of using energy – doing more with less – we will continue to race towards our double energy crisis.

The idea of energy efficiency is not new. You will be familiar with energy-efficient light bulbs – hopefully you have some installed in your home, or school. Many household appliances – refrigerators, dishwashers, washing machines and so on – now have to meet tough new energy efficiency requirements. Recycling waste heat, although not with propane, is already well established. Combined heat and power (CHP) uses the waste heat from power stations or other industry to provide local heating to offices or homes.

WHAT DO WE MEAN BY ENERGY EFFICIENCY?

Whenever energy is used, an energy conversion takes place. This means that energy is turned from one form – heat, say – to another, perhaps electricity. Every time an energy conversion occurs, some energy is wasted. The more conversions that take place, the more energy is wasted.

It makes sense, then, to have as few energy conversions as possible. Heating water by electricity requires about five energy conversions.

The manufacture and use of household appliances involves masses of energy conversions.

Heating it directly, using solar heating for example, requires only one. Even heating it by gas would require fewer energy conversions.

We could call this 'using the right energy for the job'. Electricity is brilliant stuff – we need it to run televisions, washing machines and light bulbs – but it is wasteful when we may only want to heat air or water to fairly low temperatures. In the US, nearly 80% of commercial energy is wasted, half of this in energy conversions.

INDUSTRY LEADS THE WAY

In richer regions of the world, industry accounts for more than one-third of all energy used. Most of this comes from gas, oil and electricity.

Motor-driven equipment accounts for 64% of electricity consumed by industry. To make them more efficient, motors can be equipped with controllers and variable speeds. These mean the motors match the work they need to do, and no more.

Some industries can generate up to half their own energy needs by using their own waste as a source of fuel. Even fairly simple measures, like the proper maintenance of equipment or installing insulation, can produce improvements in efficiency of up to 20%.

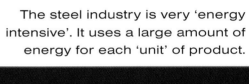

The steel industry is very 'energy intensive'. It uses a large amount of energy for each 'unit' of product.

31

GETTING BETTER AT GETTING AROUND

Earlier, we looked at the main transport energy guzzlers, which were cars, lorries and planes. A car uses nearly four times as much energy as a bus or train in carrying one person one kilometre.

Petrol or diesel-driven cars are more fuel-efficient and cleaner running than in the past. New materials make them lighter and catalytic converters remove large amounts of lead, carbon monoxide, and nitrogen gases from their exhausts. However, with the increasing trend towards four-wheeled drive vehicles and people carriers, fuel efficiency is actually getting worse. Catalytic converters become less efficient over time and do not work well over short journeys. In many parts of the world, older cars, which often do not have catalytic converters, still belt out a cocktail of poisons. The steady rise in car use outweighs many of the benefits the cleaner technologies bring.

Battery-driven vehicles are quiet, clean and efficient, but the batteries need to be charged and that requires electricity – usually produced from fossil fuels! Most of the big manufacturers are now abandoning the battery-driven car for more advanced technologies such as hybrid engines.

Another answer is to improve public transport. 'Integrated systems', like those in Sweden, mean that different types of service link up, making journeys more efficient. Switching the transport of goods from road to rail would do even more to reduce energy consumption. Unfortunately, changing habits is often harder than changing systems!

Aeroplanes use up to 11 times more energy than a bus or a train – after all, they have to get off the ground!

Car manufacturers are turning their attention to creating hybrid engines rather than battery-operated vehicles (see pages 34-39).

3,000 windows make Simmons Hall, Mass, US, a naturally ventilated building, with low-energy machinery and electrical systems making the building very energy efficient.

GETTING IT RIGHT AT HOME

Most new homes and offices in Europe or the US are now constructed to strict energy efficiency standards. Many older buildings, however, leak energy (mainly heat). The heat energy lost from the average house is the same as if there were a large hole in one of the outside walls!

Simple measures, taken by each of us, can be surprisingly effective in reducing energy losses from buildings. In 2004, a campaign was launched during Energy Efficiency Week in the UK to save energy. It highlighted five simple things people could do to reduce their energy consumption (see 'Turn it off!' below).

Turn it off!

Five things to do to reduce our energy use (UK savings in brackets):
- Turn down the thermostat by 1°C (£730 million).
- Replace ordinary light bulbs with low energy ones. (If everyone changed one light bulb in their house, the UK would save £80 million in one year.)
- Turn off televisions when not using them, rather than putting them on standby (£50 million).
- Turn off lights in unoccupied rooms (£120 million).
- Boil just enough water for your needs (£50 million).

You may be surprised at what is most effective. Most of us could stand that – it won't solve the energy crisis on its own, but it is certainly a start.

PRICE OF OIL – COST OF FAILURE

The price of oil is controlled by some of the oil-rich nations. However, the price put on a barrel of oil is only the beginning – transporting, refining and delivering the oil all add further costs and then there is the tax. All countries tax oil and some, like most European countries, add a lot of tax; others, like the US, much less. Countries like the UK reason that high fuel taxes will make people less dependent on road vehicles and persuade them to use public transport. Some believe that because governments make a lot of money from fuel taxes, it allows them to keep income taxes lower and retain their political popularity. Countries like the US think that driving a car is a question of individual freedom – it is also good for the car industry! Currently a litre of fuel costs four times more in the UK than in the US.

In 2000, roads were blocked by truck drivers and farmers enraged by high fuel prices which were causing them to lose out to their European competitors. Despite their protests, the government refused to lower the tax on petrol and diesel fuel.

The fact remains that in the UK, high fuel prices have done little to reduce fuel consumption.

ENERGY FOR THE FUTURE?

In the middle of the red dust of an old sheep station in south-west Australia is a tower. Not just any tower – this one is one kilometre tall. That's nearly twice as tall as any other building in the world; three times taller than the Eiffel Tower.
And that's not all, the tower stands at the centre of a gleaming sea of glass and plastic 7 km across.

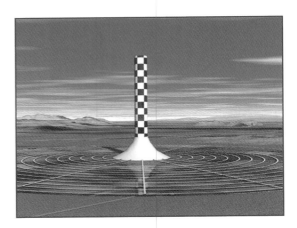

Except the tower doesn't exist. At least, it exists, but only in the minds of designers and engineers and as futuristic artists' impressions. But this does not mean that one day the tower will not soar upwards through the sky and suck up huge amounts of renewable, pollution-free energy from the Sun.

THE POWER TOWER

If it is built, the tower will be the world's biggest solar power plant. Air heated by the Sun under its giant plastic skirt will rise up the tower, turning 32 turbines and generating 650 gigawatt-hours of energy a year. That would be enough to supply 70,000 people – or a lot of industry.

The designers' vision is that solar towers will eventually provide electricity to poor nations with plenty of sunshine, but no other energy resources. Others fear the Power Tower will be a scar on the landscape, expensive to build, inefficient and vulnerable to strong winds. It may change the local climate in ways that are completely unpredictable.

Whether or not the tower becomes a reality, the search for effective, renewable sources of energy is now a matter of urgency.

Heights
Power Tower = 1,000 m
CN Tower = 553 m
Eiffel Tower = 324 m

The prototype solar chimney at Manzanares, Spain, combines three things: the greenhouse, the chimney and the turbine to generate electricity.

THE SUN ON EARTH?

We know that splitting atoms releases heat energy to drive turbines, which produces dangerous radioactive waste. Instead of splitting atoms, they can be joined in a process similar to that which powers the Sun. 'Heavy' hydrogen is heated to 100 million °C in a magnetic field. The atoms join (nuclear fusion), release energy and produce harmless helium. So far, the process has only been shown to work in the laboratory. There are plans to build a reactor, but disagreements over location and technology mean that we cannot yet build nuclear fusion into our energy plans.

HOPE FOR HYDROGEN

There is another use for hydrogen, which is shaping our ideas about our energy future – the fuel cell. Hydrogen can be burned as a fuel, but it is more efficient to convert the energy it contains into electricity. Fuel cells strip electrons off hydrogen atoms and use the electrons to create an electric current. Later, the electrons are recombined with the hydrogen and oxygen to produce water.

Fuel cells already operate world-wide. In Japan, there are over 100 plants, ranging in size from 50 kW to 11 mW. Hydrogen buses run in Iceland, and in a number of other countries. Fuel cells are pollution-free at the point of use – the only waste product is water.

This swimming pool is powered using a hydrogen fuel cell.

Enter the hybrid

It may be some time before cars powered by fuel cells are a common feature of our roads.

One drawback is the need for 'hydrogen stations' instead of petrol stations. Energy companies are not rushing to invest in hydrogen stations until they are sure vehicles powered by fuel cells will be produced in large numbers. It looks as though the immediate future may be the hybrid car. This combines a conventional petrol engine with an electric motor. The engine recharges the electric motor, which can halve fuel consumption. Hybrid car sales are expected to hit half a million in the US in 2006.

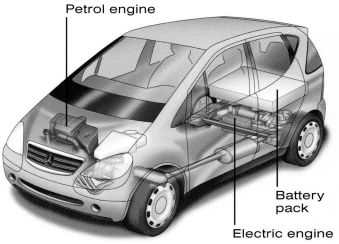

Petrol engine

Battery pack

Electric engine

The problem with fuel cells is that hydrogen has to come from somewhere. One source of hydrogen is a fossil fuel itself, methane, but this means that carbon is still released as a by-product. Another source is water! If the water can be split into hydrogen and oxygen, using renewable energy, such as wind or solar power, then the technology is still pollution-free. Of course, now we are using one form of renewable energy to produce another, but that would not matter if it were cheap or in plentiful supply. The main point is that we could free roads of the harmful effects of vehicles powered by fossil fuels.

DOWN TO THE SEA AGAIN?

In September 2003, the world's first commercial subsea (underwater) power station was hooked up to an electricity grid. The power station, anchored off the town of Hammerfest in Norway, looks like a large windmill. Suspended above the seabed, it harnesses tidal currents which turn turbines.

Now, a new generation of tidal devices are taking tidal power into the 21st century. Soon there may be 20 tidal mills off the coast of Hammerfest. The European Commission has identified 106 possible sites around Europe's coasts, 42 of them off the coast of the UK.

Most people agree we cannot afford to ignore the power of tides to meet some of our future energy needs. Developing non-damaging ways of doing this will determine how successful this will be.

The power of waves is also something we cannot ignore. As we saw in pages 14-17, the technologies involved are more challenging than for harnessing tides. It will take longer for them to become major energy generators.

A marine turbine looks similar to an underwater windmill, but instead of being driven by wind power, it is driven by ocean currents. In addition, there is no danger to fish as the blades turn slowly – around 20 times per minute.

Better than barrages!

Using tidal currents (rather than the rise and fall of tides) gets round many of the problems we saw with tidal barrages built across estuaries. Another offshore design, called a bounded reservoir, also avoids some of these problems by being built like a circular dam. Water is trapped at high tide and then allowed to escape over turbines as the tide falls. Although they use the rise and fall of the tides, they are much less damaging to estuaries than barrages. Three of these giant 'doughnuts' are currently being built off the coast of Wales.

A PLACE IN THE SUN

Many still believe the future is in solar energy by making solar cells cheaper and more efficient. Solar or PV cells have been made which can convert a whopping 36% of the Sun's rays into electricity. Currently, solar cells are only about 10-15% efficient.

World-wide, it is possible that over one billion people could be benefiting from PV electricity by 2020, 60% in poorer regions such as south Asia and Africa. By 2040, solar electricity output could be supplying over a quarter of global electricity demand.

Many countries, including the US, Germany and Japan, have programmes that are designed to ensure that solar heating and PV technology is installed in many homes and offices.

'Denim'-clothed buildings

Buildings of the future could be clothed in a flexible, power-generating material that looks like denim. Instead of the rigid silicon base used in PV cells, the material is made of thousands of tiny silicon beads sandwiched between two layers of aluminium. The flexible panels can follow the curves of buildings and the bumpy surface of the beads means the panels have a large surface for absorbing more sunlight.

BACK TO THE WIND?

For many people, wind turbines still offer the best option. Continuous improvements in design have made them cheaper, quieter and more efficient. Europe has now taken over as world leaders, producing nearly three-quarters of the world total. In the UK, about 1,000 turbines have been connected to the National Grid (although smaller scale turbines supply many local and island communities).

Windy city?

One future development could be buildings with in-built turbines (see artist's impression, below). Buildings would be constructed as curved towers which would funnel wind towards the turbines. German architects have come up with a prototype design for a two-tower 200-m-tall building with three turbines, each with 30-m-blades, slung between them. It is believed that such a design could be twice as efficient as a stand-alone wind power generator. Although wind speeds are reduced in cities, the turbines could still deliver a minimum of 20% of the building's energy needs.

37

Despite the problems of expense and danger to migrating birds, the future may be in offshore wind energy. Offshore winds tend to be higher than those on land, and larger turbines can be constructed. Long coastlines are well suited for this type of energy generation. The largest offshore wind farm in the world was completed in 2002 at Horns Rev in Danish waters. It generates enough electricity to supply 150,000 Danish homes. A report, also produced in 2002, estimated that wind power could be supplying more than 20% of the world's electricity by 2040.

The 80 turbines at Horns Rev in Danish waters are placed at water depths of between 6.5 and 13.5 m. The wind conditions at Horns Rev are so good that the offshore wind turbines are expected to produce twice the amount of energy as onshore wind turbines of the same size.

WHAT WENT WRONG WITH WATER POWER?

We have already looked at the advantages and disadvantages of large-scale hydroelectric schemes. The potential (how much could be available) is huge – enough, perhaps, to meet the entire world's electricity needs. But in both richer countries and poorer nations (with the exception of China), the rate of development has fallen behind other technologies. The richer countries are literally running out of 'acceptable' sites. In the poorer countries, investment in massive dams has not produced the growth in industry or wealth that was expected. Put simply, too much has been put into these giant schemes, with too little return.

We have seen that small-scale dams can overcome many of the problems of their larger cousins. Unfortunately, it is only in China that they make a major contribution. Governments and big investors like to put their money into large, 'centralised' projects. They are not that interested in local schemes that will still be producing power in 50 years' time, long after their investment has been paid off.

Large-scale dams have many problems which reduce their viability.

ATTITUDE PROBLEM?

This chapter has looked at some of the latest developments in new sources of energy. In one sense, there are no 'new' sources – just better, cheaper or more imaginative ways of using sources that have always existed. It remains to be seen which will eventually become the leaders in the race to replace fossil fuels. It is likely we will need them all.

Of course, we should not just look to technology to solve our energy problems. It is also a question of attitude – how we think about energy. As we saw at the start of this book, it is easy for most of us to take energy for granted – especially if we are the ones who don't have to pay the electricity bills. Maybe we need to start thinking of energy in a different way. It may not seem like it now, but usable energy is a scarce resource. We have to value it and use it wisely.

How we as individuals – and the world as a whole – might do this is the subject of the final chapter.

The attitude of today's generation, and that of future generations, could be one of the most important factors in changing the course of the potential energy crisis.

A Crisis Avoided?

In September 2004, the UK government was told by its own experts that half the country's future electricity supply would need to come from nuclear power. This was the only way, they said, the country could meet its electricity needs and keep agreements it had made to reduce greenhouse emissions. That would mean building 45 new reactors! Meanwhile, other countries were coming to similar conclusions.

The agreements the UK had made, along with many other countries, had been thrashed out in Kyoto, Japan, back in 1997. The agreement was for richer countries to reduce their carbon dioxide emissions by 5% on average compared to 1990 levels, by the year 2012. Many of the world's poorer countries were exempt from the agreement. It was recognised that they needed to develop their industries further to help their economic development. Part of the agreement allowed rich countries to 'trade' some of their emissions in exchange for helping poorer countries develop cleaner energy technologies.

The Kyoto agreement was not new – much of the work had been carried out following the 'Earth Summit' held in Rio de Janeiro, Brazil, five years earlier.

The Earth Summit in 1992 committed the world to living more sustainably. This meant limiting our use of energy.

By limiting our use of resources today, future generations will be able to benefit from them.

BACKING KYOTO

Never before had over 160 countries come together voluntarily to do something that could damage their economies – to cut down on fossil fuels. The world was beginning to accept that global warming was fast becoming a global threat.

But not everyone agreed. In particular, the US and Russia felt the evidence was not sufficient to take such drastic action. Besides, they felt the harm to their economies would be too great. Without the agreement of at least one of them, Kyoto could not be put into effect.

In October, it all changed. Due to its faltering economy, Russia's carbon emissions dropped dramatically and it could start selling its carbon 'credit'. Now it was worth Russia's while to support the agreement. Kyoto could go ahead.

Only the beginning

Kyoto was finally a success. In fact, a number of regions, including Europe, had already decided to start limiting their emissions. Some had even gone well beyond the conditions of the agreement.

But all this was only a beginning and even if all the targets set by Kyoto were met, they would do little to reverse, or even halt, the upward march of carbon dioxide. But at least the agreement showed that countries could work together when the possible future of the planet's climate was at stake.

Beyond Kyoto

So, is nuclear power the answer to rising carbon dioxide levels, as some experts are now urging? Or is it, as many others believe, a dangerous and outdated technology which should be discarded in favour of renewable technology?

Meanwhile, as the debate goes on, carbon dioxide levels go on rising. Between 2003 and 2004, it increased by a record amount and currently stands at around 380 ppm. Most scientists do not want to see it go above 450 ppm – many think 550 is more realistic. That would still mean a temperature rise of between 2 and 5°C and sea-level rises of 0.3 to 0.8 metres.

Even this limit may not be enough. A report produced in January 2005 stated the danger point could be reached when carbon dioxide levels reach 400 ppm and global temperatures increase by as little as another 1 or 1.5°C. At current rates this could be within 10 years!

LIVING WITHOUT OIL

Our world is dependent on fossil fuels, especially oil. Most estimates suggest that this will continue for the next 25 years, and possibly longer (see the chart below). By then oil may be running out and global temperatures may be rising uncontrollably.

This does not need to happen. Renewable sources of energy, particularly wind power, solar energy, biofuels and hydrogen could plug the 'energy gap'.

The benefits would be huge – an end to the massive expense and damage caused by oil exploration and extraction, less reliance on troubled regions such as the Middle East, huge cuts in pollution and a slowing down of climate change and sea-level rise.

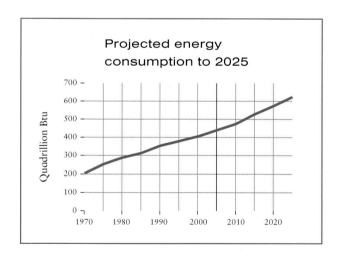

Projected energy consumption to 2025

41

Atmospheric carbon dioxide has now reached a record high.

IS IT POSSIBLE?

Studies show that simply heating, cooling and lighting buildings more efficiently could reduce energy needs dramatically. So would doubling the average fuel efficiency of cars, for example, by using hybrid engines. Increased use of wind generators and PV arrays, both directly to supply electricity grids, and indirectly to make hydrogen fuel for vehicles, would do the same. Estimates suggest adopting these measures could stabilise levels of greenhouse gases by 2050.

As well as providing energy that is sustainable and clean, these technologies would create millions of jobs and 'stimulate' economies.

The oil-producing countries would not necessarily need to suffer, either. The Gulf States are rich in sunshine as well as oil and it has been suggested that a fund could be created to help them harness this renewable source of energy.

By making buildings more environmentally friendly we could reduce our energy demands massively.

AN ENERGY STRATEGY FOR THE FUTURE?

The Kyoto agreement was a start. Now there is a new idea: 'contraction and convergence'. 'Contraction' simply means reducing the total global output of greenhouse gases. There is now agreement that a reduction of at least 60% in global emissions is needed by 2050 to keep carbon dioxide levels below 450 ppm and global temperature rises below 2°C.

This will be achieved by 'convergence'. So far, the richer countries have done most of the polluting. With convergence, national emissions will converge (come closer together). Richer countries will need to dramatically reduce their emissions, while poorer countries still have room for expansion. By 2050, every citizen of the world should be responsible for the same amount of carbon dioxide. The target would put an absolute limit on global warming.

The use of renewable energy sources, such as solar power, is one way we can reduce carbon dioxide emissions.

Putting a price on carbon

On the 1st of January, 2005, the European Union put into effect the biggest piece of environmental legislation (law) in history. It put a price on carbon. In the UK, 40% of companies, including the power companies, were told their carbon limit or allowance. If they exceed (go above) these limits, they pay!

The scheme includes 'carbon allowance trading' so that companies can also buy or sell allowances to other companies. The measures are meant to encourage them to introduce more effective energy-saving measures. Some are already doing so, but many others are not yet ready. The effect of the scheme will be reviewed in 2008.

WHERE DO WE GO FROM HERE?

At the beginning of this book we saw how global problems are often linked. Solve one and you sometimes solve another. In this case, the problems are meeting the future 'energy gap' and preventing the worst effects of pollution, especially global warming.

In the long term, renewable sources of energy could meet most of our energy needs. These will reduce our impact on the planet and replace fossil fuels as they run out. If this is to happen, governments – and society as a whole – need to take renewable energy and energy efficiency far more seriously.

There are encouraging signs that this is happening. But, even as we progress, we falter. There are already signs that some of the targets are slipping. We cannot afford for this to happen. We must make serious decisions about our energy strategy now; ones that will shape our world over the next 50 years – over your lifetime.

Making these decisions involves you. How you think, act and vote – all will count. We should never make the mistake of thinking it is for others to decide.

43

The future of life on our planet is in our own hands. If we act now it may not be too late to save the planet as we know it.

CHRONOLOGY

5 billion BC – Our Sun formed.

1.6 million BC – Early man (Homo erectus) learned how to make fire.

1500 BC – Hot springs were used for bathing, cooking and heating by the Romans, Japanese and others.

200 BC – The Chinese first began to mine coal.

100 AD – The Greek historian and priest, Plutarch, wrote about 'eternal fires' – probably a reference to natural gas.

644 – The first vertical axis windmill recorded in Iran.

1100 – Windmills were first introduced to Europe.

1300s – Hopi Indians in Arizona used coal for firing pottery. Anasazi Indians in Colorado built cliff dwellings facing the Sun, which provided passive solar heating.

1740 – Commercial coal mining started.

1765 – James Watt invented the steam engine.

1821 – The first natural gas well was drilled in New York, USA.

1834 – Thomas Davenport invented the electric streetcar (the tram).

1839 – The first fuel cell was devised by Sir William Robert Grove, a Welsh judge and inventor (but the term was not used until 1889).

1841 – New technologies made drilling for geothermal water at Larderello, Italy, economic for the first time.

1859 – The first oil-production well was drilled in Pennsylvania, USA. Henry Karl Ihrig, an engineer, demonstrated the first vehicle to be powered by a fuel cell – a 20-horse-power tractor.

1860 – Etienne Lenoir invented the first gasoline (petrol) engine.

1880 – Coal-fired steam generators were used to generate electricity for the first time.

1882 – The first hydroelectric dam was built in the Tennessee River Valley, USA.

1885 – Karl Benz invented the petrol driven car.

1887 – An American, Charles Brush, built the first automatically operating wind turbine to produce electricity.

1891 – The first natural gas pipeline was built from Indiana to Chicago, USA. It was 193 km long.

1893 – A Frenchman, Abel Pifre, designed a solar engine and used it to run a printing press.

1898 – Marie Curie discovered the radioactive elements radium and polonium.

1903 – Wilbur and Orville Wright built the first powered aircraft. The flight lasted 12 seconds and travelled 120 metres.

1904 – The first geothermal power plant (producing electricity) was built in Larderello, Italy.

1938 – Otto Hahn and Fritz Strassman demonstrated nuclear fission (splitting the atom).

1944 – The first nuclear reactor began operation in Richland, Washington, USA.

1945 – The US exploded the first atomic device near Alamagordo, New Mexico, USA.

1954 – DM Chaplin and others invented solar cells.

1973 – Oil prices rose sharply due to fears of shortages and awareness of damage to the environment caused by burning fossil fuels.

1977 – The Voyager 2 spacecraft's electricity was generated by the decay of plutonium.

1979 – A nuclear power station at Three Mile Island, Pennsylvania, USA, suffered a partial 'core meltdown' and came within 30 minutes of a major explosion.

1986 – The Chernobyl Nuclear Reactor suffered a meltdown and fire, releasing large quantities of radioactive iodine and other material.

1989 – The first international Conference on Global Warming and Climate Change was held in New Delhi, India.

1992 – The Earth Summit was held in Rio de Janeiro, Brazil; foundations of an agreement on reducing global emissions of carbon dioxide were laid down (see 1997).

1997 – The Kyoto Protocol was signed; over 160 countries agreed to cut their collective carbon dioxide emissions by 5% (compared to 1990 levels) by 2012. Daimler and Toyota manufactured the first commercial cars to be powered by fuel cells.

1998 – Buses powered by hydrogen (fuel) cells became part of the Chicago, USA, public transport system.

2001 – President GW Bush approved nuclear energy as a significant part of America's energy policy.

2003 – The worst power failure the world had ever seen struck North America reigniting fears of an impending energy crisis.

2004 – Russia finally signed up to the Kyoto Protocol, allowing the agreement to go ahead. The US refused to sign up. Four hurricanes ripped through the West Indies, Haiti and the east coast of the US, possibly as a result of climate change. Oil prices rose dramatically.

2005 – The European Union brought in carbon allowances for member countries to help meet Kyoto targets; the plan included an 'emissions trading scheme', allowing allocations to be bought and sold.

45

ORGANISATIONS AND GLOSSARY

American Solar Energy Society
2400 Central Avenue, Suite A
Boulder
CO 80301
USA
Tel: +1 303 443 3130
Fax: +1 303 443 3212
E-mail: ases@ases.org
Website: www.ases.org
The ASES promotes the widespread
near- and long-term use of solar energy.

Association for Science Education
College Lane
Hatfield
Herts
AL10 9AA
UK
Tel: +44 (0)1707 283 000
Fax: +44 (0)1707 266 532
E-mail: info@ase.org.uk
Website: www.ase.org.uk
The ASE produces resources on
energy and energy conservation,
including projects enabling students
to investigate energy use at school.

Australian Greenhouse Office
Department of the Environment and
Heritage
GPO Box 787
Canberra ACT 2601
Australia
Tel: +61 02 6274 1888
Website: www.greenhouse.gov.au
The AGO delivers the Australian
government's climate change
strategy. Its website includes ways to
save energy in the home.

British Wind Energy Association
Renewable Energy House
1 Aztec Row
Berners Road
London
N1 0PW
UK
Tel: +44 (0)20 7689 1960
Website: www.britishwindenergy.co.uk
Represents the UK wind energy
industry and promotes the use of wind
power, both onshore and offshore.

Canadian Renewable Energy
Network (CanREN)
c/o Natural Resources Canada
580 Booth Street
13th Floor
Ottawa
Ontario
K1A 0E4
Canada
Website: www.canren.gc.ca
Its purpose is to increase the
understanding of renewable energy
to accelerate the development of
renewable energy technologies.

Centre for Alternative Technology
Machynlleth
Powys
SY20 9AZ
Wales
UK
Tel: +44 (0)1654 702 400
Website: www.cat.org.uk
Produces a wide range of energy-
related resources, including
worksheets and practical kits.

Friends of the Earth (International)
PO Box 19199
1000 GD
Amsterdam
The Netherlands
Tel: +31 20 622 1369
Fax: +31 20 639 2181
Website: www.foei.org
Environmental organisation
supporting renewable forms of energy.

National Energy Foundation
Davy Avenue
Knowlhill
Milton Keynes
MK5 8NG
UK
Tel: +44 (0)1908 665 555
Website: www.natenergy.org.uk
UK charity promoting energy
efficiency and renewable energy.

Other useful websites:

www.dti.gov.uk/epa

Department of Trade and Industry
– information on UK energy
production and use by industry.

www.eia.doe.gov/emeu

US Energy Information Agency.

www.bp.com

Contains information about global
energy use and trends.

Barrages – Dam-like structures built across estuaries to trap the energy of tides and convert it into electricity.

Biomass (bioenergy) – Energy obtained from plant material, such as wood, straw, paper etc; the carbon dioxide produced by burning is the same as that removed from the atmosphere by the plant when growing.

Consortium – A group (for example, of countries), that co-operate in order to exert more control over a product or process.

Emissions – Gases, such as carbon dioxide and sulphur dioxide, produced as a result of burning fossil or other fuels.

Energy consumption – The total amount of energy used by an individual, or a country or region, over a particular period of time.

Energy conversion – Change in energy that takes place when work is done, for example, chemical energy in fuel may be changed (converted) into kinetic energy (movement) and heat in a car engine.

Fossil fuels – Fuels obtained from the fossil remains of tiny plants and animals, mainly oil, natural gas and coal; burning them always produces carbon dioxide.

Fuel cells – A way of producing electricity from hydrogen and oxygen in which the only waste product is water; producing the hydrogen may involve the use of fossil fuels, however.

Geothermal energy – Energy obtained from the natural heat of rocks.

Global warming – Warming of the Earth caused by the build up of greenhouses gases (see below); may lead to changes in climate and sea-level rises.

Greenhouse gases – Any gas, such as carbon dioxide and methane, which absorbs heat energy leaving the Earth's surface, causing an increase in the Earth's temperature.

Megawatt – A unit of power, equivalent to a million watts.

Natural selection – Process of evolution by which animals and plants better adapted (suited) to particular conditions survive and pass on their genes to future generations.

Nuclear fission – Splitting atoms and using the heat energy released to produce steam in order to drive turbines; the technology underlies all nuclear power stations as well as the development of some atomic weapons.

Nuclear fusion – Joining atoms of 'heavy' hydrogen together at high temperatures to generate energy in a process similar to that in the Sun and thermonuclear devices (the hydrogen bomb).

Oil-based economy – A country or region whose economy depends heavily on oil and other fossil fuels to meet its domestic and industrial needs.

Passive solar heating – Using the Sun's heat directly, normally to heat water in solar panels or lagoons, or in constructing buildings so they make maximum use of the Sun's rays.

Renewable energy – Energy, such as wind and solar power, which is not used up when we exploit it; often less polluting than other (non-renewable) forms of energy, such as fossil fuels and nuclear power.

Solar cells – Specially treated panels that enable the energy from the Sun to be converted into electricity (also known as photovoltaic or PV cells).

Sustainable development – Using resources, such as energy, in such a way that we do not prevent future generations from also gaining the benefits of those resources.

Turbine – Any mechanism, usually with blades, that is turned by steam, water, wind or other source of energy. Turbines are attached to generators which produce electricity.

INDEX

48

Photo Credits:
Abbreviations: l-left, r-right, b-bottom, t-top, c-centre, m-middle. Front cover: t, b, mr, ml; Back cover: t, b — Photodisc. Front cover mc — Flat Earth. 3tr, 33t — Arup. 4 — Associated Press. 37br — BDSP Partnership. 28b — Nicolas Benazeth. 16b — http://bioenergy.ornl.gov. 1m, 42bl, 42br — BioRegional. 12 — British Nuclear Fuels plc (BNFL). 15t — www.bp.com. 14t — Aaron B Brown. 16 (both) — www.calpine.com. 1l, 2tl, 18, 23tr — Comstock. 6b, 26br, 31tl, 41b, 43b — Corbis. 7, 42t — Corel. 14b, 22, 27br, 39t, 40b, 44bl — Digital Vision. 2-3, 38 (both), 45tr — © Elsam A/S. 34tr — EnviroMission. 2bl, 20, 32l, 40t, 44t — © European Community, 2005. 43tl — European Parliament. 1r, 9, 23bl, 31br — Flat Earth. 10bl — www.greenhouse.gov.au. 36t — Marine Current Turbines Ltd. 35tr — www.mercedes-benz.com. 24 (all), 27t — NASA's Earth Observatory. 15b, 21, 35b — PBD. 5, 8, 11, 17t, 19, 25, 26tl, 29b — Photodisc. 6t, 10t, 13, 33b — Select Pictures. 32r — courtesy of The Lind Group. 30t — US Department of Energy. 37t — Zapotec Energy, Cambridge, Mass., USA.